READ YOUR WAY TO FENWAY

This book belongs to:

RED SOX FOUNDATION

Bank of America

MAYOR THOMAS M. MENINO

THE BOSTON PUBLIC LIBRARY FOUNDATION

D1530032

Fenway Park!

Created by the Red Sox Wives Organization for Red Sox fans of all ages!
Proceeds will benefit children's charities supported by the Red Sox Foundation

BARNES
&NOBLE
BOOKS

NEW YORK

Thank you for purchasing **Fenway Park 1∗2∗3**. My husband, Red Sox principal owner John Henry, and everyone in the Red Sox organization knows how fortunate we are to have such an extraordinary group of men as players and coaches for the Boston Red Sox. Equally extraordinary are their wives—women who match their spouses' dedication to our team with their own efforts on behalf of children. This new book is an example of their ongoing commitment to Boston's many local charities and to the Red Sox Foundation.

Fenway Park 1∗2∗3, as well as **Fenway Park from A to Z**, published in 2002, was created by the Red Sox wives to raise much needed charitable funds. They have selected The Jimmy Fund at the Dana-Farber Cancer Institute, Children's Hospital—Boston, and the Children's AIDS Program at Boston Medical Center as beneficiaries of the proceeds from the sale of **Fenway Park 1∗2∗3**. Each of these exceptional nonprofits represents a lifeline for children throughout the world, many of whom travel to these renowned centers for treatment. We are honored to support them.

We hope that you will share these charming books with your family and friends and join us in saluting the efforts of the Red Sox wives. Their commitment and your generosity will make a world of difference to children in need. We are proud to have the Red Sox wives—and you—on our team.

Peggy Henry

One Fenway Park

Did you know Fenway Park was built in 1912?

SLUGGER

Two Red Socks

Did you know the Red Sox have been wearing red socks since 1907?

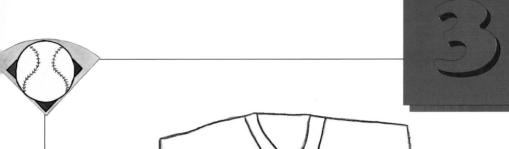

Karen Varitek
'04

Three Red Sox jerseys

Did you know each player has 3 Red Sox uniforms? White is for home games, red is for Sunday games and gray is for away games.

Four of Wally's favorite ice cream flavors

What is your favorite kind of ice cream?

BOSTON
BOSTON AMERICANS
1903
WORLD SERIES
CHAMPIONS

BOSTON RED SOX
1912
WORLD SERIES
CHAMPIONS

BOSTON RED SOX
1915
WORLD SERIES
CHAMPIONS

BOSTON RED SOX
1916
WORLD SERIES
CHAMPIONS

BOSTON RED SOX
1918
WORLD SERIES
CHAMPIONS

Lisa Kapler '04

Five World Series

Did you know the Red Sox have won 5 World Series?

1903, 1912, 1915, 1916, 1918

6

Hall of Fame
Bobby Doerr
1985
#1

Hall of Fame
Joe Cronin
1956
#4

Hall of Fame
Carl Yastrzemski
1989
#8

Hall of Fame
Ted Williams
1966
#9

#27
Hall of Fame
Carlton Fisk
2000

Hall of Fame
Jackie Robinson
1962
#42

Six retired players' numbers hang in Fenway Park

Do you know the 6 retired numbers?
#4 Joe Cronin, #1 Bobby Doerr, #27 Carlton Fisk, #9 Ted Williams,
#8 Carl Yastrzemski, #42 Jackie Robinson (a Brooklyn Dodger)

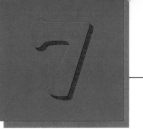

Seven innings means it's time to stretch

Everyone sings "Take Me Out to the Ball Game" during the seventh-inning stretch. Do you know the words?

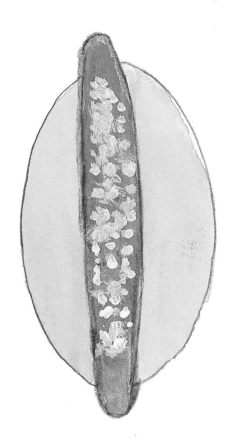

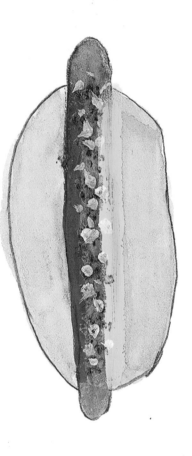

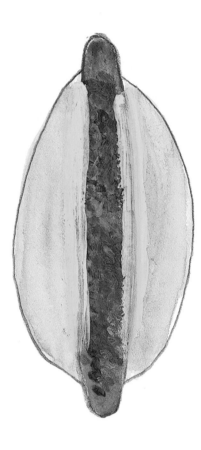

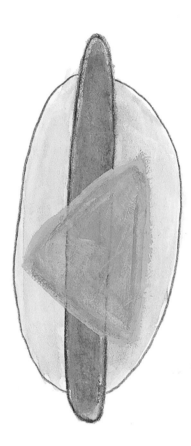

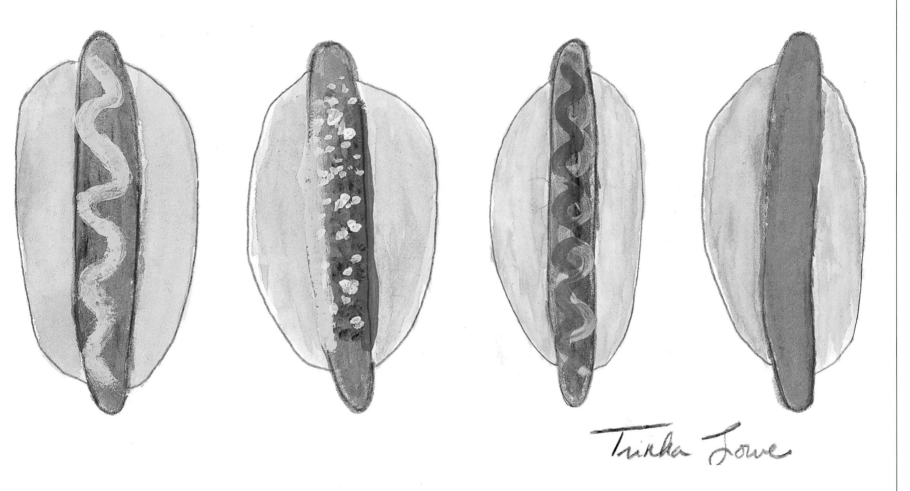

Trinka Lowe

Eight Fenway Franks

What do you like to put on your Fenway Franks?

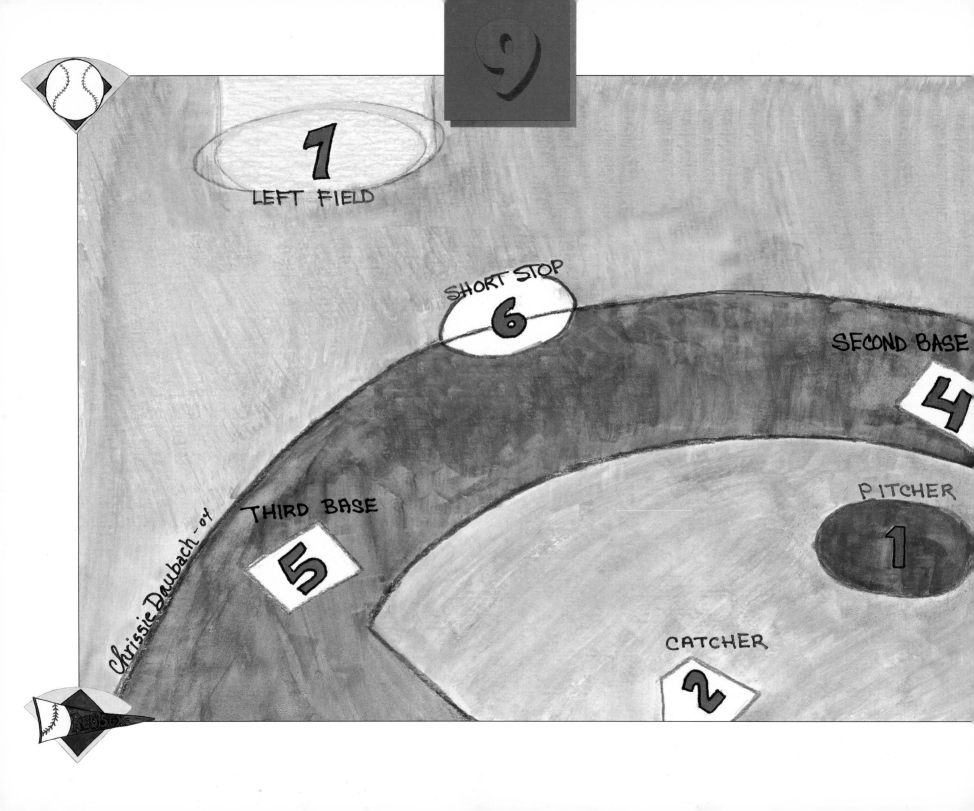

Nine positions on the field

Can you name the 9 positions in baseball?

CENTER FIELD

RIGHT FIELD

FIRST BASE

monica McCarty '04

Y PARK

Ten letters in Fenway Park

Can you name any other baseball stadiums?

Eleven baseball caps

Did you know that there are more than 11 styles of
baseball caps at Fenway Park?

Melanie Embree '04

Twelve baseballs in a box

Do you know that official baseballs are made of leather?

Thirteen stripes
on the American Flag that flies at Fenway Park

Did you know that the 13 stripes on the flag
represent the 13 original American colonies?

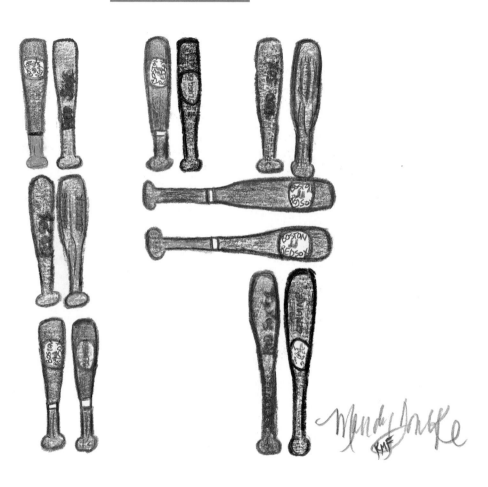

Fourteen bats

Did you know that each player has his own special bat?

BAT

SOUVENIR HAND

BALL

CUP

SHORTS

BATTING GLOVE

FLOPPY HAT

GO RED SOX!

FLAG

KEYCHAIN

SIGN

SOCKS

JERSEY

WALLY DOLL

BOBBLE HEAD DOLL

HAT

Jeana Millar
2004

Fifteen Fenway souvenirs
Do you have a favorite souvenir?

Kristen L. Mirabelli '04

Sixteen pieces of equipment
Do you know what each piece of equipment is used for?

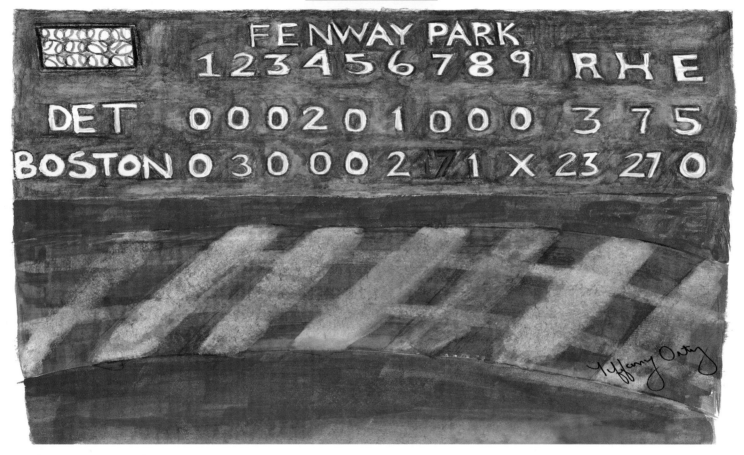

Seventeen is the most runs scored by the Red Sox in a single inning so far

Did you know that the Red Sox scored 17 big runs in a game with Detroit at Fenway Park in 1953?

Eighteen is the number of players' feet when the Red Sox are on the field

Can you count 18 red socks?

Stacy Wakefield

Nineteen peanuts in a bag

Did you know that peanuts are more popular than popcorn at Fenway Park?

Twenty fans at Fenway Park

Did you know that people come from all over the world
to visit Fenway Park?

All drawings are by Red Sox Wives

1

Lisa Williamson—**number One**

6

Marta Rojas—**number Six**

2

Shonda Schilling—**number Two**

7

Beth Rowe—**number Seven**

3

Karen Varitek—**number Three**

8

Trinka Lowe—**number Eight**

4

Kathryn Nixon—**number Four**

9

Chrissie Daubach—**number Nine**

5

Lisa Kapler—**number Five**

10

Monica McCarty—**number Ten**

11

**Aimee Arroyo
& Sarah Anderson—number Eleven**

16

Kristin Mirabelli—number Sixteen

12

Melanie Embree—number Twelve

17

Tiffany Ortiz—number Seventeen

13

Dawn Timlin—number Thirteen

18

Michelle Damon—number Eighteen

14

Mandy Foulke—number Fourteen

19

Stacy Wakefield—number Nineteen

15

Jeana Millar—number Fifteen

20

**Juliana Ramirez
& Susan Leskanic—number Twenty**

Red Sox Players

The Red Sox Wives
thank those who made invaluable contributions to
Fenway Park 1★2★3.

The Art Experience
Avon, MA
Art supplies

Elaine Ostrander
Felos Art Center, Stoughton, MA
Cover artist and advisor

Nancy Corbett
Felos Art Center, Stoughton, MA
Artistic advisor

Liz First-Raddock
Copy editor

Jane Dickson
Barnes & Noble Community Relations
Prudential Center, Boston, MA

Leonard Vigliarolo
Cover and interior book design

Debbie First
Advisor to the Red Sox Wives Organization

A heartfelt thank you to **Meg Vaillancourt**,
Dr. Charles Steinberg, **Vanessa Leyvas**
and **Kerri Moore** of the Boston Red Sox

And a special thanks to the Boston Red Sox and Red Sox Foundation

2

10 4 16

6 18

1

13 9

17 11

15 12

7

19 3 8

5

14 20